BORN TO WIN

Lynne Palmer

Published by
**STAR BRIGHT
PUBLISHERS**

ISBN 0-9709498-2-0

First Printing 2002

Published by:

Star Bright Publishers
2235 East Flamingo Road
Suite 300-D
Las Vegas, Nevada 89119
Phone: (702) 369-4026
Fax: (702) 894-9918
Toll Free: (800) 615-3352
Web Site: www.lynnepalmer.com
Email: starbrite@softcom.net

Cover Design by Marcia Snow

Printed and bound in the United States of America

CONTENTS

INTRODUCTION

Gambling is nothing new — it's been going on for many centuries. People gambled by playing with dice, similar to Craps, more than 5,000 years ago in ancient Mesopotamia. From there it spread to Greece and Egypt. Dice games became so popular that in the time of the Etruscans, they were brought to Rome. Julius Caesar enjoyed playing dice as well as the Roman soldiers. In about 750 A.D., an Arabian dice game was popular in Corsica, a French island in the Mediterranean. Soon dice games (craps) became the rage throughout Europe, and eventually spread to other countries. However, in many European countries today, Craps is not played because the people don't know how to play it, or have lost interest in it and are consumed by Slots, Roulette, Blackjack, or Baccarat.

The theory is that Roulette originated in China, although, there are many people who believe it was first played in France. It's rumored that a monk invented it due to boredom with his life within the quiet walls of the monastery. Roulette is played all over the world. The American and European table layouts differ, but the game is similar, regardless, of where Roulette is played.

During the Han dynasty in China, Keno was created. Lottery and Keno have many similarities. Mexico, Germany, Malta, and many other countries all over the world have been playing Lotto. Mexico has had a lottery system for over 60 years. Canada and the United States have had Lottery-mania now for decades. Many of the lucky winners are now millionaires, especially those who have followed Gail Howard's amazing lottery formulas. (Try it yourself FREE by visiting her Web Site at www.gailhoward.com or call Toll Free 1-800-945-4245 for information about her books and software.)

In the early 1890's Video Poker had its origins out of coin-operated gaming devices. These poker slot machines have evolved, especially with the age of electronics — they are computer generated. By 1979 they became more sophisticated when the 701 Draw Poker machine was introduced. Now there are all types of Video Poker machines — The Joker is Wild, Deuces Wild, Progressive, Double-Up, Bonus Poker, Double Poker, Double-Double Poker, and Loose Deuces, Triple Poker, etc.

Sports betting has been going on since ancient times: In Rome it was the chariot races, in Greece it was the Olympics. In Mexico, Jai Alai, cockfights, and greyhound racing are popular. In the United States, and other countries, people wager heavily on horse and harness racing. Basketball, baseball, football and other games are bet on. Even when golfers play a round, they bet among themselves. People spend money gambling in pool halls when they play billiards. Poker games and tournaments are popular. Bingo is played in many churches, as well as for benefits. Private bets are made between people in just about everything imaginable — thus, gambling is here to stay.

The games with the worst odds are Keno, Lotto, and the Wheel of Fortune. The best odds are given in craps, baccarat, blackjack, poker and dollar slot machines.

It is best to avoid betting amounts of money that make you lose control. Do not bet on a sports game just because the game is being televised. There are two types of bettors: one treats it as a business, is unemotional, and knows when to quit; the other bets for the sport of it, is emotional, and does not know when to quit, especially if it is the home team in a sports game.

When you gamble, plan to spend an amount that you can afford to lose — do not spend beyond that. Do not borrow money if you are on a losing streak. Do not pawn your furs, jewels, or other possessions. Use self-discipline. Do not get carried away thinking you can make it back.

When you are on a losing streak, stay away from all forms of gambling. Winning goes in cycles — you cannot win every night. Often there are long periods of winning or losing. If you have your horoscope done by an astrologer who is well versed in gambling charts — then you'll know when you are on a winning or losing streak (cycle). If you're in a casino, and get a gut feeling you'll lose — then quit and go home.

When you gamble, you take a risk. It's a chance that maybe you'll win. You are never sure of the outcome, until the game is over. Gambling provides entertainment and is stimulating; the adrenalin shoots up with your excitement. Often your expectations are not the final result, which is a real "let down" (downer).

While you are gambling, you should realize that it is your money you are risking in this chancy investment. You want an investment that'll yield a profitable return. Think of it as if you are buying a house, a business, playing the stock market, or investing in bonds or gold. These are all forms of gambling. Put aside a certain amount and call it "entertainment" money — once you lose that — quit! If you can't stop, you may discover you've got "gambling fever." For most people gambling is a fun game — entertainment. But for the compulsive gambler, it's not just a game — it's an emotional illness. It's an addiction that does not stop even when everything is lost — money, work, and loved ones. Stress and emotional frustration escalates as the gambler tries to get even; deeper and deeper into debt the compulsive gambler goes, until nothing is left. If you have planets in Scorpio (or according to your horoscope Scorpio or Pluto rules your gambling house) — it's best that you stay away from gambling. Scorpio and Pluto represent addictions. If you've been infected with "gambling fever," call "Problem Gamblers Help Line" at 1-800-522-4700 (available 24 hours a day, 7 days a week).

I live in Las Vegas, Nevada — the gambling capital of the world. I have witnessed people lose their homes, savings, jobs, loved ones and families. The casino's are in business to make a profit — and they do. They make money from the compulsive gambler, but can lose to a disciplined gambler. Some signs of a person with "gambling fever" are: difficulty in stopping or losing control — the urge to gamble is all the person can think about; borrowing money, especially using credit cards to go into further debt. A compulsive gambler takes time off from work to gamble, or may not be home much with family — they neglect themselves and shirk responsibilities in order to wager their last cent. They may not tell the truth about the money, and time they spend on making a bet. When you gamble, it is best to set aside a sum of money and tell yourself, "This is what I can afford to lose, and if I lose it, I will quit." If you do this, but renege on your promise to yourself — this could indicate a gambling problem. So, nip it in the bud right away — be persistent and don't lie to yourself or let yourself down. Be proud of yourself when you are able to stop. Walk away and think of your lark as "entertainment" — just as if you spent it at a sports game or going to the theatre.

In 1994, a man from London' arrived in Las Vegas with $220,000, which took him a few years to save. He made arrangements with Binion's Horseshoe Casino to allow him his own private roulette wheel so he could wager the entire $220,000 on one roll of the wheel. (Most casinos do not allow bets this large.) He placed the money on the color red and won! He quit and went back to London with $440,000! He knew when to quit and Lady Luck was certainly smiling at him.

There was a handicapped man who appeared on the "People Are Talking" TV show in Baltimore, Maryland which was co-hosted at that time by Oprah Winfrey. The man attributed his winning the Million Dollar Lottery to the advice I gave on the same show a month earlier. I have had many winners, such as Joyce Vincent, when she won the Wingo newspaper contest on August 6, 1982 in New York City. The prize was $50,000, which she has to share with four others. Others won following my gimmicks, numerology systems, or because I forecast it by looking at their horoscopes. Many people, I never met won huge amounts of money based on my books or listening to me give gimmicks on radio or television shows.

Hourly there are millions of winners worldwide in Lotto, keno, craps, bingo, slots, poker, baccarat, roulette, blackjack, horse and dog racing, Jai Alai, sports betting and many more games of chance too numerous to mention. Those people who are lucky enough to win have favorable aspects in their horoscopes. Also, they have gambled on a day that was lucky for them according to numerology. Or they won on a slot machine that was a lucky number for them (the machine's model number when added was broken down to a one or two digit number). That number was based on numerology (see Chapter Three).

A winner is confident; a loser is negative. Your attitude is shown by the harmonious and discordant expressions of the planets and signs of the zodiac (see Chapter Two). Often intuition, gut feelings, ESP (Extra Sensory Perception), first impressions or a hunch pays off — in other words, follow your instincts (sixth sense). Many lottery winners stated that they won because they picked the winning numbers by random choosing. Others won because they chose numbers that were lucky for them, i.e., theirs, or another's birthday — and unbeknownst to them, the numbers were probably lucky according to astrology and numerology. Or what about the huge amount of people who won because they followed Gail Howard's Lotto systems? Her systems are scientific formulas; over 74 first prize Lotto Jackpot Winners won over 97 million dollars — try it yourself FREE by visiting her Web Site at www.gailhoward.com.

What about those winners who believed that the rabbit's foot they carried with them brought them into the winner's circle? Or those who said their lucky charm, talismanic gem, gemstone or piece of jewelry was rubbed and wished on — thus they won the lottery or a casino jackpot (see Chapter Five). Whichever method is used, and if it works for you, that is the system to use. After all, "Magic is in the believing." And, I am a firm believer that anything you can do to improve your luck — is the best route to take.

Regardless of the method used to win, you cannot win if it is not in your horoscope to win. (A horoscope is based on your day, month, year, time and place of birth.) It's also possible that your horoscope has favorable dates to win, but you didn't. Why? It could be many reasons, such as: you wore a gemstone or piece of jewelry that's unlucky for you; you chose unlucky numbers (based on numerology and the astrological correspondences); you were not in a casino that was lucky for you; you played a slot machine whose model number was unlucky for you; you didn't follow your psychic ability; you were in an unlucky numerology day for gambling; you were negative or couldn't concentrate on the game or video poker machine; you didn't do your best with blackjack because your hit went over 21, or you should have let it stand, instead of having a hit.

I have won in Craps, roulette or on video poker machines (the only games I'll play). I am an analytical observer, who has spent endless hours, in casinos analyzing the slot machines. I have stood behind a row of players at the slot machines and studied the sequences that came up on the machines (regular slots as well as video poker). I try to think like a computer programmer (the machines are computer-generated) who keeps you in the game through teasing you into believing you are going to be a winner. I can watch a machine that is being played and can tell whether the person playing will win or lose. There is a pattern that is easy to discern, if one is unemotional and analytical. In this book, you'll learn the secrets that I've learned from years of experience. I hope Lady Luck is smiling in your direction. Bet to Win! Good Luck!

Lynne Palmer

CHAPTER ONE
ARE YOU A LOSER OR WINNER?

PORTRAIT OF A LOSER

In astrology Saturn is the planet of loss, when expressed on the negative side. If you use the discordant side of Saturn, even if it is for a day, week, month or year, you should NOT gamble. Those who are born with a strong Saturn usually do not like to waste time or money on gambling. But there are certain planetary aspect times when discordant Saturn traits are activated in your horoscope.

If you feel, act or think like any of the following characteristics, avoid gambling. Some of the negative Saturn traits are used when a person lacks confidence, complains, worries, cries poverty and can't get over a loss. The Saturn personality is insecure, fearful, doubtful, full of anxieties, overly cautious, afraid to take chances, self-destructive and feels pressured to make money to pay the bills. As a rule this person is serious, seldom smiles and is an introvert or a loner. Others see this individual as a bad sport.

PORTRAIT OF A WINNER

In astrology Jupiter is the planet of gain (or winning), when expressed on the positive side. If you use the harmonious side of Jupiter, even if it is for a day, week, month or year, you could gamble and win. Those who are born with a strong Jupiter usually enjoy taking risks and do not fret or get upset if they lose. There are certain planetary aspect times, when harmonious Jupiter traits are activated in your horoscope.

If you feel, act or think like any of the following characteristics, you could be a winner. Some of the harmonious Jupiter traits are used when a person laughs, jokes with others, spreads cheer and is confident. The Jupiter personality is secure, jovial, friendly, gregarious, outgoing, easy-going and has fun. This Jupiterian person is an extrovert. Others see this individual as a good sport, even if a loss occurs. This type of individual treats loss with an "Oh well, that's life! You can't win every time. I had a great time even though Lady Luck was not smiling at me." Usually, this person is a winner; however, a person can lose if the day (according to numerology) was not lucky for gambling, or the casino was not lucky (based on numerology — the casino's address; or, according to astrology, the horoscope of the casino clashed with the individual's horoscope). But as a rule, the preceding types of behavioral traits are what constitute a winner.

CHANGE YOUR ATTITUDE

Life is constantly changing — nothing stays the same. So, why shouldn't you make some changes so you'll become rich through winning a lottery or jackpot? Do you want to start a Lucky Streak so you can be happy and satisfy your heart's desires? Are you getting what you want out of life? Do you know that half the battle is in believing in your dreams and knowing that they can come true?

Write down where you want to be, figure out how you'll get there, and then tell yourself you are going to do it, regardless of how long it takes. Picture yourself living your dream — visualization is an important key to success. If you see yourself achieving your goals, you're on the way to realizing them.

Avoid negative people. Follow your gut instincts. When you have failures, setbacks and obstacles thrown in your path, realize that this is NOT the time to give up. These negative occurrences only serve as stepping-stones to make you strong. Learn from mistakes and get on with your life. Never be a quitter. Persevere. Think of problems as a test of your strength. If you are able to get through them, you can get through anything. Keep your course straight when you're on the road to be a winner.

Do not have doubts, complain, worry or get depressed — these thoughts will defeat your purpose such as going for the gold. Reach for the good (brass ring) — think only of the good. Do not dwell on the past. Know that persistence is the number one key to success. Believe in yourself. Have faith that everything is in divine order.

A winner is strong and never lets go of his/her dreams. If you have a setback, find another angle, a fresh approach and open a new door. Perhaps, you may need to wear a gemstone or piece of jewelry that's lucky for you. Or use numerology (see Chapter Two) for your lucky numbers. Use positive Jupiter thoughts, and, gamble only when you're in a Jupiterian frame of mind. When you try again with a positive approach, you are very likely to reach your goal. For it is knowing that unless you try again, you may lose your opportunity to be successful.

So by now you know that your mental attitude is the main key to success. Believe in your own power, and your potential for prosperity — thus, this secret power that comes from within your soul, can help you get your heart's desires. Be enthusiastic. Be optimistic. If a negative thought creeps into your mind, say, "Erase that thought — out — out you go!" Make these positive forces part of your daily life and, thus, you'll be a winner.

CHAPTER TWO
WHAT KIND OF
A GAMBLER ARE YOU?

In astrology there are twelve signs in the zodiac. Your horoscope is based upon the day, month, year, time and place of your birth. There are eight planets — Mercury, Venus, Mars, Jupiter, Saturn, Uranus, Neptune and Pluto — and two luminaries — the Sun and Moon — in our solar system, as we know it. These planets (and luminaries), as they appear to us in the sky, are located in one or more of the twelve signs of the zodiac, which are situated in the various constellations. Your Sun sign is the sign that the Sun is in at the exact moment you are born. You have an inner power that, when applied, allows you to control your outer environment. The inner power is represented by your Sun and/or *dominant* side when used on the positive side.

Each of these ten elements — eight planets and two luminaries — will occupy a sign of the zodiac. Thus you may have different signs of the zodiac in your horoscope. If a zodiacal sign is close in degrees to the other zodiacal signs in the horoscope it may be considered *dominant* and if there is more than one planet in a zodiacal sign, that zodiacal sign may also be considered *dominant* in your horoscope and, thus, is the key to your character. In other words, if one zodiacal sign is close in degrees to the other zodiacal signs, or if more than one planet is located in a zodiacal sign then you will act more like this zodiacal sign than any other.

If your Sun sign is not your dominant sign, you may not express its traits. Perhaps you have more planets in another zodiac sign and therefore that zodiac sign is more *dominant* than your Sun sign. If this occurs, you may be aware that you are constantly expressing the characteristics of this *dominant* sign and *not* your Sun sign. It's very possible to have several zodiac signs that are *dominant*. When this happens, you act and think like the traits representative of each zodiac sign that is *dominant*. That is why many people say, "I am not at all like my Sun sign, therefore, I don't believe in astrology."

As the earth turns on it's axis, a particular zodiacal sign appears on the horizon at the exact hour, minute, and second of birth — it is "rising" or "ascending" in view and, thus, is called the Rising or Ascendant sign. Perhaps, you're more like your Rising sign than your Sun sign if the Rising sign is *dominant* in your horoscope.

The type of gambler you are can be determined by reading the traits of these zodiacal signs and planets. If you discover you are using mostly the harmonious traits, then you are expressing the harmonious side of the zodiacal sign or planet. However, if you are using mostly the discordant traits, then you are expressing the discordant side of the zodiacal sign or planet — thus, when you feel those inharmonious traits arise — DO NOT GAMBLE, because you could lose.

You are expressing ARIES or MARS *harmonious* traits if you *win* because you are daring, gutsy, make quick decisions, and are willing to take a risk. When you play, you feel the adrenalin rush to your head. Gambling is an exciting adventure as you spend money fast, regardless of the cost. When you become a jackpot winner or leave the blackjack table with lots of cash, you can hardly wait until tomorrow when you'll try your luck again.

You are expressing ARIES or MARS *discordant* traits if you *lose* because you are impulsive, impatient, and impractical. You get too carried away with the excitement of gambling; thus, you take unnecessary chances — often wild ones with your money. If you don't win fast enough to suit you, it won't be long until you leap from one slot machine to another or from one blackjack table to another. You'll spend your last cent on gambling. The gambler in you wants a big stake; however, it's the thrill of winning that is more important to you than the dough. When you lose, you get angry, walk out of the casino waving your hands in the air and muttering that the slot machines are rigged or the blackjack dealer did some tricks with the cards. You're not a quitter; you'll be right back as soon as you've got cash to blow away.

You are expressing TAURUS *harmonious* traits if you *win* because you are conservative when you gamble; you bet small amounts at one time on blackjack, the lottery, and roulette. You do not bet the maximum amount on slot machines — only one coin at a time. You've set aside a certain sum — when that's gone you quit. You're not a risk-taker, but use common sense. When you win, you do not continue to play, because you're aware that the odds of continual winning are against you and on the side of the casino.

You are expressing TAURUS *discordant* traits if you *lose* because you believe you won't win. Inwardly you have a fear of losing money, and, since thoughts produce things — you wind up behind the eight ball. When someone rushes you, your stubbornness shows. If you play blackjack, (due to a slow mind) you lose, because you can't think fast enough to decide whether you should stay with the cards you hold, or be hit with another card.

You are expressing GEMINI *harmonious* traits if you *win* because you think fast, make good decisions, and will quit playing on one machine (if it isn't paying off fast enough for you) and play two machines simultaneously. And don't you feel great when both machines pay off at almost the same time? You're mentally stimulated by taking chances with roulette, blackjack, and slot machines — you believe in diversification and will take a chance and buy lots of lottery tickets too. You feel that by so doing, your odds to win will improve.

You are expressing GEMINI *discordant* traits if you *lose* because you're confused and vacillate — "Should you play this machine or that machine? Or should you write down this number or that on your lottery ticket? Or, when playing blackjack, should I stand or hit with the cards? Or, with roulette, which numbers should I play?" Your mind becomes so confused that, also, you can't keep tract of what you are doing and may hit the wrong buttons on a video poker slot machine. Your nerves jump with the noise in a casino; you can't sit still for long and could be winning and just walk out the door. Or perhaps, you lose your lottery ticket or can't remember where you placed it.

You are expressing CANCER or the Moon *harmonious* traits if you *win* because you followed a hunch when choosing numbers for the lottery or roulette table. Your gut feelings told you which slot machine to play. However, you must be in the mood to gamble; the thought of taking a risk is exhausting. Often, you'll fluctuate between wanting to, or not to, play a video poker machine. Once you've won on a particular machine, you'll feel that that is "my machine." Thus, every trip to the casino, you'll return to that lucky slot machine.

You are expressing CANCER or the Moon *discordant* traits if you *lose* because you're an emotional gambler. Frustration sets in when you play a video poker machine that fluctuates — one moment you're way ahead, the next moment you've lost everything. When playing the lottery or roulette, your mind wavers relative to the numbers you should play. Money is easily lost because it was difficult for you to make a decision, especially when playing blackjack. The losses come faster when you work yourself up to a tizzy — that's when the tears flow.

You are expressing LEO or the Sun *harmonious* traits if you *win* because you bet to win — your positive, strong, power thoughts come to the fore. You think big, are a high roller, and will buy twenty lottery tickets (or more) at one time. Perhaps, you play the five, or one hundred dollar, slot machines. You wouldn't stoop to playing the penny, nickel or quarter machines — you want enormous returns on your money and think it's fun to take a risk. When playing roulette or blackjack, you'll play for higher stakes with twenty-dollar (or more) chips. You think of yourself as a winner and when you win big, everyone will know about it as you bask in the glory of applause or the publicity you receive.

You are expressing LEO or the Sun *discordant* traits if you *lose* because you overextend yourself with enormous spending habits. It's difficult for you to control the urge to gamble with large sums of money. Credit card debt doesn't even faze you. You enjoy showing off, especially when people tell you that you're one of the last of the big-time spenders. The gambler in you remarks, "If I don't take a chance, nothing can be gained." The risks you take make others shudder, although, some people are in awe of you – that makes you glow. If methods to improve your gambling are suggested, your ego won't allow you to listen. You don't get upset when you lose; in fact, losses are ignored as if they don't exist. You blame everyone, but yourself, when you lose.

You are expressing VIRGO *harmonious* traits if you *win* because you use common sense, logic, are practical and have analyzed the slot machines. Facts, figures and statistics are studied; you want to know your best odds to win and, therefore, stay away from blackjack, roulette and the lottery. Your analytical mind thinks like a computer, and the slot machines are computer generated, so before you play you observe others playing all over the casino. You watch the cards coming up on the video poker machines and can easily figure out which machine will pay-off. When you play a machine, you won't hit the buttons until you've thoroughly analyzed all the cards. Once you win, you know when to quit.

You are expressing VIRGO *discordant* traits if you *lose* because you're afraid to take chances, thus, sit on your money and feel that every hand dealt on the video poker machine, or in blackjack, will be unfavorable. You don't trust the roulette ball to land on your number, black, red, odd, even, etc. Your negative thought that "I never win," works against you. Gambling to you is a waste of time and money. You are overly cautious and could quit the moment you've lost a few dollars. You're a cheap gambler who can get lost in the details and not see the overall picture.

You are expressing LIBRA *harmonious* traits if you *win* because you weigh the pros and cons, before playing. Gambling to you is fun, an amusement that perhaps can bring enormous rewards when you hit the jackpot. You feel that you're lucky — more so than most people. The risks and gains are exciting. The money you win is a ticket to the good, luxurious life you yearn for. You don't spend too much, or too little, on games of chance — many call you a conservative gambler. Because your zodiacal sign is ruled by the Scales, you make sure your checkbook and pocket money are evenly balanced.

You are expressing LIBRA *discordant* traits if you *lose* because you are indecisive — "Should I hold or cancel this card on the video poker machine or in blackjack, should I stand or be hit?" Also, losses occur because you're easily influenced by others; perhaps, someone gave you bad advice on a game you played. If you're in a spending mood, you'll go broke trying to win. It's easy for you to get greedy; you don't know when to stop. Often, you'll drive yourself crazy weighing the pros and cons when gambling; such as, "Should I play roulette, blackjack or a slot machine?" The lottery has so many numbers to choose, it's too over-whelming for you — thus, you take your chances and pick just anything while thinking, "I should not play Lotto." But the money gained for winning the jackpot is tempting — it can give you the leisurely life you enjoy. Thus, you'll give in and play.

You are expressing SCORPIO or Pluto *harmonious* traits if you *win* because you are resourceful, check everything out thoroughly before playing. You'll see what slot machines have already paid off, so, will stay clear of them. You'll look to see which video poker machine pays off the most money. The progressives are for you. You probably took a notebook and watched others play; thus, with your computer-mind, you have a good idea how a machine was programmed. Once you've studied sequences and the escalation up and down of a machine, you'll chance it, if you're first impression tells you to "go for it!" You excel at testing machines; gambling is mentally stimulating. You're a good card counter when playing blackjack. You've got the famous "poker face" that most gamblers envy. You have a positive attitude that you'll win, especially when you apply your research findings. Your investigative mind can make you a winner!

You are expressing SCORPIO or Pluto *discordant* traits if you *lose* because you can't control the obsessive, compulsive urge to take a risk in games of chance. When you're hooked, you can't let go — you do not know when to quit. You keep coming back for more to get even, regardless, of the cost. You'll do anything to win, even go into credit card debt, pawn something, sell a home, spend every dime you have from your paycheck, ignore loved ones and gamble as if you're possessed by a demon. You are persistent and block everyone and everything out of your mind. You are a controller; however, gambling controls you.

You are expressing SAGITTARIUS or Jupiter *harmonious* traits if you *win* because you're optimistic, confident, enthusiastic, guided by your feelings and feel that you're lucky. You believe the skies the limit as to the enormous sums of money you can win. You're a high-roller who laughs outwardly and think that you're having a great time — this is stimulating and fun, entertainment. You enjoy taking risks. You tell yourself, "It is only money — either I make it big, or not at all. There's more money where that came from, if I lose." Your belief is that all paths leading to gambling are like streets paved with gold. When you win, everyone can see how happy you are, especially if you jump up and down and exclaim loudly, "I've won!"

You are expressing SAGITTARIUS or Jupiter *discordant* traits if you *lose* because you're overly optimistic, overly confident and take wild chances on sheer impulse. You leap from one machine to another, without stay-

BET TO WIN *BY LYNNE PALMER*

ing very long; thus, you don't give the machine a chance because if you don't win immediately — you're off and running. You laugh your way from one loss to another. You'll buy loads of lottery tickets. You'll play almost every number on the roulette table, simultaneously. You splurge, think big and disregard the true value of money. Your motto is "Easy come, easy go." When you go home broke, you're not upset. As a loser, you're a good sport. You'll say, "Next time I'll win. I had a wonderful time gambling, and that's all that counts, isn't it?"

You are expressing CAPRICORN or Saturn *harmonious* traits if you *win* because you are thrifty, practical, patient, cautious and spend only that which you can afford. You bet small amounts; penny and nickel slot machines may be to your liking. You'll pick the machines that pay off regularly. Slot machines that payoff big amounts are shunned; you believe that the Draw Poker and Bonus poker machines pay less money but pay off more frequently than the Double Double Poker machines. You go more for a "sure thing." You know when to quit and go home with a profit, be it a small or large sum of money.

You are expressing CAPRICORN or Saturn *discordant* traits if you *lose* because you're depressed, negative, worried about money, insecure, overly cautious and lack confidence. You don't trust the blackjack or roulette dealer. You are suspicious of the machines — thinking that the casino has set them so you'll lose. You think it is impossible to win the lottery because the odds to win are too great. You believe you're unlucky at gambling. You're a poor sport and lose sleep over losses. Your greed to keep winning more makes you lose it all. You don't know when to quit.

You are expressing AQUARIUS or Uranus *harmonious* traits if you *win* because you are intuitive and follow those sudden lightening-like flashes that pop into your head. You select a machine at random and are in shock when you've hit the jackpot. You thought you were losing, only to discover you won. It all happens so fast with you. Roulette is played automatically, without picking numbers on purpose; often, you win playing the red, black or over and under numbers. Blackjack is played by making spur-of-the-moment decisions. Lotto is played by picking numbers on the ticket where your pen lands; often, you don't even look until afterwards to see the numbers you selected. You know when to quit gambling; in a jiffy you're out of a casino.

You are expressing AQUARIUS or Uranus *discordant* traits if you *lose* because your systems and theories don't pan out. You look at your notebooks and are stymied why certain numbers didn't make you a winner while playing roulette. Your "I-know-it-all" attitude can cause losses, especially when an expert points out your mistakes. You are obstinate and won't budge an inch for anyone, even if the person is right. Your spur-of-the-moment gambling whims appear to others to be a careless way of spending your dough. You are too erratic and unpredictable when it comes to gambling, either you are too tight or you'll squander every cent you have.

You are expressing PISCES or Neptune *harmonious* traits if you *win* because you are a psychic gambler who follows your ESP to win. You believe that you will win, thus, you'll bet to win. You're a high roller who thinks if you spend a lot, you'll make a lot. Lots of lottery tickets are purchased at one time. Slot machines with the biggest payoffs are played. You use your sixth sense when you guess which numbers the roulette ball will land on. You can visualize yourself winning; you've got an active imagination and can just see that jackpot prize or the lottery check with millions coming to you. You believe in Lady Luck and feel that you are blessed as a lucky gambler.

You are expressing PISCES or Neptune *discordant* traits if you *lose* because you are a foolish and impractical gambler. You're a real risk-taker who later worries over your losses and indebtedness. You are an emotional player who wholeheartedly believes that you'll win; it's an enormous disappointment when you lose — a real heartbreak that leaves you crushed. Listening to wrong advice can make you lose; hot tips make your eyes go big thinking about all that money you're going to win. You don't know when to quit, perhaps, you've got a video poker machine up to a large amount — but you think it'll go higher. When it starts to go down, you think it will go back up again — finally, it takes you all the way out and, then, you've lost everything. You throw good money after bad money, but you can't help yourself — because you look at everything through rose-colored glasses.

You are expressing MERCURY *harmonious* traits if you *win* because you are mentally alert, sharp, astute, incisive, sensible, using good reasoning and logic. You're able to communicate your ideas readily. Your memory is excellent. You are informative, interested in formulas and tend to be adaptable and flexible. Successful decisions are made.

You are expressing MERCURY *discordant* traits if you *lose* because you are confused, disoriented, preoccupied, mentally changeable, lack continuity, indecisive and make wrong decisions. You tend to be high-strung, nervous, restless, jumpy and can't sit still for very long. You have difficulty when communicating with others.

You are expressing VENUS *harmonious* traits if you *win* because you think of gambling as fun, entertaining, amusing and a good way to socialize — especially, when you are playing blackjack or roulette. You tend to be easygoing, kind, pleasing, light-hearted and, thus, profit from having a good time.

You are expressing VENUS *discordant* traits if you *lose* because you are readily influenced by others when choosing a slot machine, numbers in the lottery or on a roulette table. You are easily tempted to gamble and throw money away. You take the easy way out and give in to the line of least resistance; perhaps, because you're in a lazy mood — you walk to the nearest slot machine, regardless of whether someone just won on it or it doesn't have large payoffs. Or you don't change machines because it takes too much energy to move from one to the other, especially when you're comfortable sitting where you are.

CHAPTER THREE
NUMEROLOGY AND WINNING

Do you know about the "Secret of Numbers?" As far back as ancient times people used numbers for various things. According to C. C. Zain in his book *"The Sacred Tarot,"* (published by the Church of Light), the ancient system of numbers dates back to the Jewish Kabala, Moses, Abraham and Adam. The Kabala which contains the Hermetic System of numbers was originally passed through allegorical stories from Adam to Noah, Abraham, the Egyptians, Moses, David and Solomon. It was finally in written form at the time of the destruction of Solomon's second temple.

Translators, C. C. Zain discovered, made use of the equivalent letters but they had no knowledge of the vibratory rate it contained since they were not versed in astrology or the occult. But through the years, other systems of numerology and astrology grew out of the original one; thus, today, you will find many different versions used by a range of people. But those who were involved in the occult used the original numbers throughout the ages.

Pythagoras (a Greek philosopher, theologian and mathematician) discovered the relationship of numbers to individuals and their fate (destiny). However, he was not versed in astrology, thus the Pythagorian number system differs from the Hermetic one. I have used the Hermetic System of Numbers since 1957 and find them to be more accurate than any other system of numbers. Those versed in numbers believed they had magical powers that could help or influence others. In the ancient days, gambling was popular among the common people as much as those in royal circles. Numbers were meant to be good or bad omens, depending upon the user.

The seven centers of the ancient world (Egypt, Crete, Chaldea, India, China, Mexico and Peru) combined astrology and numerology. The signs of the zodiac and the planets represent different types of thinking. There are 12 signs and 10 planets — thus, there are 22 numbers that correspond to these planets and signs of the zodiac.

At all times, you are tuned in to a particular vibration (lucky or unlucky), which is ruled, by a sign and/or planet and its corresponding number. When a number is thought about, that thought is definite energy radiated toward you or a thing. Now you can understand why it is important to use numbers that are lucky for you. To win, you need Lady Luck and Lucky Numbers. Use the numbers which follow when gambling: Add up the model number on a slot machine, the casino's building (address) number, or when playing roulette or Lotto. The table that follows (Astrological Correspondence to Numbers) contains 22 numbers, which correspond to a planet or zodiacal sign.

TABLE: ASTROLOGICAL CORRESPONDENCE TO NUMBERS

1 = Mercury	9 = Aquarius	17 = Gemini
2 = Virgo	10 = Uranus	18 = Cancer
3 = Libra	11 = Neptune	19 = Leo
4 = Scorpio	12 = Pisces	20 = Moon
5 = Jupiter	13 = Aries	21 = Sun
6 = Venus	14 = Taurus	22 = Pluto
7 = Sagittarius	15 = Saturn	
8 = Capricorn	16 = Mars	

ADDING NUMBERS

If you are adding a number on a slot machine (the model number which can be found at the side, back or top of the machine), or you are adding numbers above 22 to play on a roulette table or in the lottery — break any number over 22 down to a single or double digit number that does NOT EXCEED 22. The following numbers are an example of how to break down numbers (add the numbers, then break down):

31, 40, 103, 121 — *break down to 4, Scorpio*

23, 32, 41, 50, 104, 122, 131 — *break down to 5, Jupiter*

24, 33, 42, 51, 60, 105, 123, 132, 141 — *break down to 6, Venus*

25, 34, 43, 52, 61, 106, 124, 133, 142 — *break down to 7, Sagittarius*

ZODIACAL SIGNS AND PLANETS: DISCOVERING YOUR LUCKY SIGN, PLANET, NUMBER

To determine whether a zodiacal sign's, or planet's number is lucky for you is dependent upon your habitual, or momentary (at the moment you gamble) pattern of thought and action. Read both the harmonious and discordant side of the zodiacal sign and planet (Chapter Two), and ask yourself, "Was I lucky or unlucky (did you win or lose) at the time I felt and acted this way?"

Often your thoughts are a mixture of more than one planet or zodiacal sign. In that case, you could be vibrating to more than one number (planet or zodiacal sign).

If you *won* while expressing the traits of a planet (planets) or zodiacal sign (signs) then, when you gamble, you could be lucky with the number (numbers) they correspond to. Use these numbers for the lottery, roulette or slot machine (its model number).

For example: You're laughing and in a happy frame of mind. You are confident that you'll win. If you don't, your attitude is, "Oh, well, you can't win all the time. At least I had a great time." That type of thinking is of a Sagittarius or Jupiter nature. Sagittarius (on the Astrological Correspondences to Numbers Table) corresponds to number 7, and Jupiter corresponds to number 5. Thus, those numbers (and what they break down to — single or double digit) are numbers to use for roulette, Lotto, or the number (model) on a slot machine.

Let's say you are going to play the lottery and choose six numbers; you could choose 5, 25, 32, 41, 43, and 50. These numbers correspond to both Sagittarius (25, 43) and Jupiter (5, 32, 41, 50). Actually in astrology Sagittarius is the luckiest zodiacal sign and Jupiter is the luckiest planet. Or you want to play roulette — then you could play many numbers (more than with the lottery) if you choose which correspond to Jupiter or Sagittarius.

If you *lost* while expressing the traits of a planet (planets) or zodiacal sign (signs) then, when you gamble, you could be unlucky with the number (numbers) they correspond to. *Do not use these numbers* for the lottery, roulette or the slot machine's model number. In fact, if you are in this discordant frame of mind — it is best to stay away from gambling.

For example: if you are confused and your mind jumbled up (Gemini or Mercury discordant traits), do NOT gamble. Perhaps, you go to the casino and once there cannot decide whether you should play a certain slot machine or maybe you should play blackjack or roulette. It's best to stay away from gambling and especially do not go to a slot machine that has a number 1 or 17 model number. Do not play these numbers with roulette. Do not go to a casino whose address is number one or number seventeen. Do not play these numbers, when your thoughts are scattered (indecisive) with the lottery. It is best for you to save your money and gamble when your mood changes.

CHAPTER FOUR
USE YOUR PSYCHIC ABILITY TO WIN

Everyone has psychic ability, but many people are unable to recognize it when it happens. Neptune, and the sign Pisces, rule *ESP* (Extra Sensory Perception); Uranus, and the sign Aquarius, rule *Intuition;* Pluto, and the sign Scorpio, rule *First Impressions;* The Moon, and the sign Cancer, rule *Hunches and Instincts.* Any of these zodiacal signs, or planets, could be involved when you are gambling.

When *Uranus,* or *Aquarius,* is involved — Intuition is used. If, suddenly, something pops into your mind, like a flash of lightening from out of the clear blue sky — that's Intuition, especially when you did not previously think about it. Perhaps, it occurs when you're picking lottery numbers or numbers to play in roulette. Or it could be a slot machine that catches your eye, especially from afar, or even close by. Aquarius Intuition is used when you say the words, *"I know,"* such as: *"I know* I'm going to win." *"I know* I must play that slot machine over there." *"I know* I should play these numbers in roulette or with the lottery." *"I know* I should take another card" (when playing blackjack) or *"I know* I should NOT take another card." Heed your inner voice, especially when you say, *"I know."*

When the *Moon,* or *Cancer,* is involved — Hunches and Instincts are used. Your gut reaction is giving you a tip, which, if followed, could make you a winner. Cancer

Hunches and Instincts are used when you say the words, *"I feel,"* such as: *"I feel* I'm going to win." *"I feel* I must play that slot machine over there." *"I feel* I should play these numbers in roulette or with the lottery." *"I feel* I should take another card"* (when playing blackjack) or *"I feel* I should NOT take another card." Your *Feelings* could make you rich.

When *Pluto*, or *Scorpio*, is involved — First Impressions are used. It's as if an inner urge compels you to follow a certain direction. These First Impressions are strong, compulsive (almost obsessive) and seem to drive you take action, regardless of the cost or if anyone tells you not to do it. Scorpio, and Pluto, First Impressions are used when you say the words, *"I must* bet on these numbers (Lotto, roulette)." *"I must* play that slot machine over there." *"I must* take another card" (when playing blackjack) or *"I must* NOT take another card." These First Impressions could put you in the winner's circle; however, be careful — see Chapter Two, Scorpio-Pluto discordant expressions.

When *Neptune*, or *Pisces*, is involved — ESP is used. Pay attention to your dreams when you're asleep. Follow your Third Eye (psychic point on the face, sixth sense; also, called "mind's eye") — you'll receive a visual effect like watching a movie. It's almost as if you are inwardly creative and using the imagination to the fullest. If you want to tune in through meditation then: lie down, close your eyes, relax and breathe deeply. Ask God, or a higher-than-human power, to guide you toward making the right decision. Visualization could appear like a dream, especially if you're in a trance-like state. Perhaps, you'll see numbers (to bet on) or a picture of the casino you should go to. Maybe, you'll see a large check, or bundle of cash being paid you.

When you enter a casino, and want to play a slot machine, stand by the entrance and look at the entire room.

The slot machine that first catches your eye is where you should play. If someone has already won on it, try it anyway. Many slot machines pay off over and over again; others seldom, if ever, pay off. If you change your mind and go to another machine, you could lose — it's your first instinct, hunch, impression, thought or intuition that's the most accurate. Do the same for picking a roulette or blackjack table. If you are picking numbers to play for roulette or the lottery, do not swerve (change your mind) from the numbers you FIRST WANTED TO PLAY. Do not be afraid to tune in to your inner self. Who knows? You may find the pot of gold at the end of the rainbow if you listen to your psychic ability. It's worth a chance, isn't it?

CHAPTER FIVE
THE POWER OF GEMSTONES AND JEWLERY

There are certain gemstones that are worn as jewelry that are lucky, or unlucky, for the wearer. If you are expressing the *harmonious* traits of a certain zodiacal sign, or planet, then the gemstone that corresponds to that sign, or planet, is most likely to *bring you luck*. If you are expressing the *discordant* traits of a certain zodiacal sign, or planet, then the gemstone that corresponds to that sign, or planet, is most likely to *be unlucky for you*.

Gemstones, and crystals, have rare powers and have contributed to good fortune for the people of today as well as those in ancient Rome and Greece. You can boost your chances of winning by tapping into the power of gemstones or crystals. However, when wearing them, it's important that your attitude is positive. These gemstones and crystals are capable of transmitting and absorbing energy — thus, if you are negative, you are better off not wearing them. Each gemstone (or crystal) has a different vibration (zodiacal sign or planets expression) that channels bioelectricity from your mind and body — thus, you could have a valuable aid if you want to be a winner. They can become extensions of your being and help you to amplify, focus and release harmonious energy (thoughts and actions) in a powerful way.

Look at the following table of Zodiacal Signs and Planets to see which gemstone could be lucky for you. (Be sure to read Chapter Two for the zodiacal signs, or planets, on their discordant side.)

TABLE: ASTROLOGICAL CORRESPONDENCES TO GEMSTONES

ARIES:	Amethyst, carnelian, rose quartz, red opal, red spinel
MARS:	Red stones, brimstone, ocher, pyrite
TAURUS:	Moss agate, white coral, alabaster, white opaque
GEMINI:	Beryl, Alexandrite, chrysoberyl, aquamarine, agate, striped stones
CANCER:	Emerald, Moonstone, green tourmaline, malachite
MOON:	Silver
LEO:	Ruby, amber, cat's eye, crysolite, girasol (fire opal), hyacinth, adventurine, ruby spinel
SUN:	Gold
VIRGO:	Jasper
LIBRA:	Diamonds, white quartz
SCORPIO:	Topaz, bloodstone, lodestone, vermilion, harmatite
PLUTO:	Black diamond (uncut)
SAGITTARIUS:	Red garnet, turquoise, stones with red and green mixed
JUPITER:	Jade

CAPRICORN:	Onyx, sardonyx, jet, black opal, black tourmaline, smoky quartz
SATURN:	Jet, Black stones
AQUARIUS:	Blue sapphire, asteria, jacinth, blue opal, blue tourmaline, lapis lazuli, blue spinel, sapphirine, black pearl
URANUS:	Stones that are dazzling white, chalcedony obsidian
PISCES:	Pearl, peridot (olvine), pearly white opal
NEPTUNE:	Mother-of-pearl, iridescense pearl
MERCURY:	Quicksilver setting
VENUS:	Yellow opal

To *increase* your *psychic powers,* wear, hold or keep in your living quarters these stones: Aventurine, clear quartz, Moonstone. To *increase good fortune,* wear, hold or keep in your living quarters these stones: Aventurine, clear quartz, malachite, jade. However, keep in mind that if these stones are not lucky for you, as mentioned before (see Chapter Two, discordant expressions of the planets and zodiacal signs and their corresponding gems in this Chapter — Five), then do not wear them.

INCREASING YOUR GEMSTONES POWER

Relax; let your mind flow freely over the money you want. Visualize yourself as a winner and owning the amount of cash desired. Hold the stone, gemstone or piece of jewelry in one hand — slowly let it go over your body (without touching yourself). Start with your feet and work your way up to the head. This action draws negative energy out of the body. While moving the stone or piece of jewelry over your body, say, "Erase all negative energy from my physical body and mind."

Meditate, take slow, deep breaths and concentrate on winning. Put strong feeling and emotion into your thoughts. Feel as if you've won, the money (or check) and it is in your hands as of now — visualize and say that to yourself. Devote ten minutes a day, for three days, to performing the preceding. Do not let others touch or hold your gemstone or piece of jewelry — you do not want their vibrations on it, especially, if they tend to be negative. Do not tell anyone about this ceremony. Often, others, innocently, do not see you as a winner or having a lot of money.

Wear or carry your lucky gemstone, or piece of jewelry, with you, especially when you're gambling. If you play Lotto, or buy a lottery ticket: rub your lucky gemstone or piece of jewelry before, or while, you're picking numbers... and say, "Make me a winner!" If you go to a casino, rub your lucky gemstone, or piece of jewelry, while sitting and playing at a slot machine. If you are going to play roulette or blackjack, rub your stone, or piece of jewelry, while playing or just as you approach the table. Mentally say, "Bring me good luck. Let me play the right numbers and make the right decisions to win big."

When you gamble, keep in mind that winning comes from within — self-directed energy. Project with lots of power — feel that the world is yours and sense that everything is working together to help you find that pot of gold at the end of the rainbow.

CHAPTER SIX
LUCKY BELIEFS
OR SUPERSTITIONS?

Folklore fantasies are common to many cultures and are passed from generation to generation. For centuries these beliefs, superstitions or old wives tales have been bandied about and practiced by many. They are still "in" today and performed by all types of people around the globe. Who hasn't heard of the "medicine man" in various tribes? Or what about the elves and leprechauns who enchanted the

Irish? They believed that the leprechauns sat on a pot of gold. Many see a rainbow and "wish upon it," but has anyone ever tried to follow it to the end? What about kissing the blarney stone in Ireland — belief, myth or what? I've kissed it, so, I guess I now have a "gift of gab."

These folklore fantasies are ways to get your wishes granted, without having to work for them. Is it wrong to hope that these "little people," such as the Irish elves or the Norwegian trolls, are going to bring us our heart's desire? What about the children who believe that Santa Claus is going to bring them what they want? And how many people carry a rabbit's foot, or wear an elk's tooth on a chain around their neck, for good luck?

A hundred years ago it was customary for the French to send greeting cards on April 1st. The cards had fish as their central motif, accompanied by other good luck symbols such as horseshoes, pansies or the four-leaf clover. Those who pick a four-leaf clover are supposed to have luck — a belief that came from Ireland and spread around the world. The adage, "To be in clover," means that you're prosperous. There are those who believe that if you eat cloves or cinnamon in your food that, as those spices enter your body, you are charged with positive energy to attract riches. In ancient magical rituals, the following is said to attract money: fern, Irish moss, Irish dill, honeysuckle, skullcap and valerian. The Druids in ancient England believed that mistletoe brought wealth, when they cut it down from the oak and let it fall on a piece of clean, fresh cloth. Some people carry Tonka beans in a purple bag so they'll be lucky and wealthy.

In some cultures it is believed that if you pat a nightclub hostess on the bottom, that her good luck will be used up; however, if you burn her accidentally with a cigarette — that's good luck. In Bodrum, Turkey, the natives buy Good Luck Stones in stores, shops and at flea markets; ask for a "mazar boncugu" and watch your luck change. In Poland, Asian countries and the United States, people collect and display elephant trunks raised high — it's a symbol of good luck. The ivory or green jade is collected by those who can afford it. Many people wear them as a talismanic charm or piece of jewelry.

In Tokyo, nightclub owners put a little pyramid of salt by the door to make clean business; others do it in the United States to bring money in the door. What about those who believe that if you spill salt, you should throw it over your left shoulder for good luck? Or did you know that some people are so superstitious they won't enter a room, home or apartment unless they put their right foot first — then you'll attract good luck. There are many who believe that if you break a mirror, you'll have seven years of bad luck.

Have you ever wished you had a magic lamp so you could rub it and out would pop the genii granting you your every wish? The Brazilians believe that if you catch a one-legged boy under glass that he'll (his name is Saci) will make your wishes come true. The Chinese celebrate their New Year with many traditional symbols which they believe bring good luck, such as: the home filled with narcissus, crab and fish, fish-shaped ornaments, tiny Buddha statues, jade pendants, red rear-view mirror charms, bright red "Lucky Money" envelopes with a small amount of money inside, red diamond-shaped paper used as stationery. The ancient art of Feng Shui, based on Chinese folk wisdom, is used. A constant flow of water in your home, or place of business, brings money. If you have bamboo in your home, you'll attract prosperity.

Most people know that if you place a horseshoe over your door with the open end up (so luck won't spill out), you'll attract wealth. Bubbles in your coffee means you're going to get money; also, when your left hand itches, expect money to soon come flowing in. If you want to be lucky, look at a New Moon over your left shoulder. Throw coins in a fountain and make a wish. It seems that in every culture, all over the globe, there are those who have their beliefs and superstitions. By many, it's called "magic." According to the dictionary, "Magic is the belief that man can coerce nature by use of certain rites, formulas, actions; it can be found as an element in all primitive religions. It is an over-powering influence that proves irresistible or extraordinary."

Does "magic" work? I would answer, "Yes," because I and others who have followed my "magical devices" have attracted money or other things yearned for. In many of my books and appearances on radio and television, I have given my "check gimmick." The results have been phenomenal: a man in Baltimore won a million dollar lottery after hearing me tell the audience how to do it on "The People Are Talking" television show, co-hosted by Oprah Winfrey. Countless others have received money from gambling, newspaper contests, sweepstakes, rebates and many other forms too numerous to mention. How long has this been going on? I would say, that I have given my "check gimmick" to others since the late 1960's.

You may ask, "How does it work?" From antiquity to modern times, man has discovered that the mind is the highest type of active agent to bring you the images you want. Human actions are directed by the mind and, thus, can bring human events such as winning the lottery, hitting the jackpot in a casino or winning big stakes in roulette or blackjack. Once a magic ritual is performed, it's important to release it (don't think about it any more). By letting go of the thought-energy, your desires have a chance to manifest. Be patient. Remember, "Magic is in the believing. Thoughts produce things." Mentally say, at the end of a ritual, "I fully and freely release this positive energy into the ethers so it can work in my behalf. So shall it be!"

The best time to do "magic" is in the wee hours of the morning. The best days are: Sunday (for power),

Thursday (for great wealth) or Friday (a Venus day — Venus represents "ready cash"). When you perform magic, make sure you express an Intense Emotional Charge of Desire Energy. Use your imagination and visualize your having received whatever it is that you're asking for.

You must use mental effort, consciously or unconsciously, to attain your desires. Thus once your mind has set a wish into motion, it can be more easily and quickly granted than if you left it purely to chance. Sit back and think about, through visualization, the things you want — that you feel "I must have." Is it to win the lottery, a jackpot at the casino, a home, furs, jewelry, a car, designer clothes, to put your children through college or to travel? If there is a lottery drawing, visualize your winning — do it the night before the ticket is to be drawn. Call on the angels (everyone has many angels around them as well as the special "guardian angel") to help you. Or pray to God to make you a winner.

When you are meditating, or performing your "magic" ritual, *believe* and *know* that you can make your dreams come true and that patience and determination can make them happen. Look to every day as a day of new beginnings, open your mind to positive action and unlimited sums of money. You could tell yourself, "I am rich. I won the lottery!" Or you could say, "Bring me a million dollars." "Bring me great wealth." Let me win the jackpot at the casino." You could say any of these things while holding an object such as, a piece of jewelry, gemstone or even actual cash in your hand.

My "check gimmick" is given in my books *"Money Magic"* and every year in my annual *"Astrological Almanac."* I will give you a brief synopsis of how it is performed: If you do not have a checking account, you can do the "check gimmick" on a piece of paper (draw a form of a check). Make the check payable to you, or the name of a business you own. On the line (of the check) between your name and the signature, write: Paid in Full.

On the signature line (where you normally sign your name), write The Law Of Abundance. Do NOT put a date nor an amount on the check. If you do, you'll limit your receiving money to that date and that amount. Do not void the check stub or you'll void the check. The idea is that The Law of Abundance is going to pay you in full an unlimited sum of money forever (because you did not date the check). Fold the check, place it in your wallet or check-book and forget about it. If you change bank accounts, redo the check. The best time to do the check is two days after the New Moon, thus, your money increases, as does the Moon when it increases in light.

Give thanks for an immediate and complete payment of the money you desire. Thank God or the angels or a higher-than-human power for bringing you your heart's desire. Isn't it wonderful to know that your "magic" ritual can help make you rich?

CHAPTER SEVEN
LOTTO — THE LOTTERY

According to the dictionary, "Lotto is a game of chance played by drawing numbers from a container and covering with counters the corresponding numbers on cards, the winner being the first to cover a row of num-bers." "Lottery," according to the dictionary "is a game of chance offering money or prizes in which tickets are distributed or sold, the winning ticket, or tickets, being secretly predetermined or ultimately selected in a chance drawing. An activity or event regarded as having an out-come depending on fate." Furthermore, the dictionary states, "Any matter in which the likelihood of success is uncertain: Marriage is a lottery."

Lotto is played all over the world; the numbers in a game vary from country to country as well as from state to state in the United States of America. The odds to win are unbelievably high, especially when there are lots of numbers to select in one game, and there are a million or more people playing a game. I have clients who, not only play in their home state, but also play in Germany, Canada and other states in the United States of America. The lower your odds, the better your chances are to win, even if it's a small amount and not the millions you can win in the bigger lotteries. It's best to win something and not to get greedy. However, it's worth taking a chance on the "biggie" lotteries; perhaps, you'll win so much you'll be a multi-millionaire.

Many lotto players do not realize that their chances to win are slim. Those who have consulted with me, cannot understand, even when I explain it to them. I tell them that the winner has to have a lucky horoscope, better than anyone else's. So what do you do to win? I believe you should try everything in your power to win. Perhaps, you should play the "Pick-3," "Pick-4" or "Pick-5" numbered games. The less numbers in a game to select from, the better your chances are to win. For example: If you have 49 numbers in a game and must pick six out of 49 numbers — that's difficult; however, if you have 25 numbers in a game, and picked six out of 25 numbers — that's much easier and improves your odds to win.

Many lotto players, and some have won big, continually play the same numbers every time a game is played. They believe that there is a better chance for those numbers to be drawn over a long period of time. There are those players who choose numbers because of their, or a loved one's birthday. Others select numbers based upon an important event that transpired in their life. People have all sorts of reasons why they pick certain numbers. I know individuals who picked numbers because they dreamed of those numbers.

There are certain planetary configurations that you have to have in your horoscope to win. Jupiter is the planet of wealth, therefore, when you win millions of dollars, you need to have an aspect in with Jupiter. Also, you need aspects with Uranus or Neptune — if Jupiter is involved harmoniously with one of these planets, your chance to win is heightened. But how many people, playing the same game, have these planets activated at the time of a drawing? Many, but those who win chose numbers that were lucky for them.

If you've read the previous chapters in this book, you are then aware of the various techniques you can do to improve your chances to win. However, I will briefly outline them for you:

1. Never choose numbers when you are doubtful, depressed, worried, or negative about anything — those traits are the attitude of a loser (see Chapters One and Two).

2. Wear, or hold, a gemstone or piece of jewelry that is lucky for you at the time you are picking numbers (see Chapter Five).

3. Choose numbers that are lucky for you according to numerology (see Chapter Three).

4. Use your psychic ability when selecting numbers to play. If you *Feel* that you'll win by choosing six numbers out of 25 — go for it. Pick numbers at random, if you know you can rely on your psychism (see Chapter Four).

5. To improve your chances to win do my check gimmick or indulge in one (or more) of the folklore fantasies (see Chapter Six). For example: you know the date and time the lottery numbers will be drawn. Therefore, hours before the drawing — and while watching the numbers being drawn on television — use STRONG, INTENSE EMOTION and mentally say, "Let numbers — (state your numbers) be drawn. Make me a winner!" At the same time visualize those numbers to be the

BET TO WIN *BY LYNNE PALMER*

winning numbers. Also, visualize yourself appearing on television holding up your check. However, do not visualize the amount on the check, because it could be more than you visualize.

In my opinion, Gail Howard (see Introduction) is the foremost lottery expert in the world. Therefore, if you want to increase your odds of winning the lottery, even further than I've outlined, visit her Web Site at www.gailhoward.com and use her FREE interactive systems that have won two, or more, first prize jackpots.

CHAPTER EIGHT
SLOT MACHINES

BEFORE YOU PLAY A SLOT MACHINE

Do not play if you are doubtful, depressed, worried or feel desperate to make money to pay the bills. If you play while feeling these emotions, you'll probably lose. Only play when you're in a confident mood (see Chapters One and Two). Pretend that playing a slot machine is your chosen form of entertainment; instead of going to a movie or sports game, you're going to a casino.

Figure out how much money you can afford to lose. Set aside a certain amount of money to play with; treat it as your budget. Do not take credit cards with you to the casino; take only the cash you are going to play with. If you win, and are satisfied, don't go for more. Be disciplined; know when to quit — avoid being greedy. Be thankful when you win. If you lose, don't go chasing after the money hoping you can make it up. If you do, you're a compulsive gambler, and could continue to lose — then what kind of rut would you be in, financially? If you are on a losing streak, return another day — perhaps, then Lady Luck will smile at you. Winning and losing goes in cycles; you can't win every hour or every day in a row. The longer you stay at a machine, especially if it's not that great paying off, the more money you'll put back into the machine.

When you enter a casino, from the distance (near the entrance), look at the entire room filled with slot machines. The slot machine that stands out (catches your eye) is, perhaps, the best machine to play. As you approach the machine, visualize winning on that machine. Say to yourself, "You're going to make me a winner." Many people perform rituals when they play a machine. Some pray; others wave their hand, over the slot machine's screen, mumbling something not audible to anyone else's ears.

What if, when you are looking over a room to see which slot machine you want to play and you don't have a feel for any machine in the room? Perhaps, you should go to another casino, if one is available in your area. Perhaps, you'll lose. Or you can walk around to the various slot machines, look for their model number at the top, back or sides; add up these numbers (see Chapter Three) and see if that number is lucky for you. Usually, the best machines, for the majority of people, add up to a five (you break down the numbers until your final number is a five — 14 is not broken down to five, but anything over 22 is). A number that adds up to a Five corresponds to the planet Jupiter — the luckiest planet in astrology — it rules LOTS OF MONEY, ABUNDANCE, and WEALTH. If you are in a cheerful, happy mood, perhaps, the number Five machine will make you a winner, because Jupiter represents riches and confidence. (Note: For all planetary and zodiacal sign numbers, feelings and thoughts — see Chapters Two and Three).

There are tight and loose slot machines. Those tight machines (many people call them hungry — hungry for more money to be put in them) are set to pay off in small amounts (little rewards or value for your money) from time to time — and sometimes never pay off. The loose machines pay off big and most of the time. There are some machines that are set to continually (almost) pay off. If you are a daily visitor to the casino, you'll know which machines pay off and which don't — be analytical when studying the machines; think of it as a business — do not let emotion rule.

It is important that you keep in mind that slot machines (regular and video poker) are computer generated. Each machine has a random number generator and a computer chip that selects the number, card, cherries, double diamonds, 777, etc., and what it pays. It's smart to check the payoffs before playing a machine. Certain casinos have machines that pay off better than other casino's machines. Often a dollar has a better pay off (higher) than a quarter or nickel machine. It takes a lot of nickels to make much money. The progressive machines pay off big, but not as frequently as other machines. However, it's dependent upon how many people play that machine over and over again — naturally, the more people who continue to play one machine, the better chance it has to pay off. Usually, it is wise to play in an area (or row) where many machines have, or are in the process of, paying off. Those areas keep paying off over and over again. Stay away from those slot machines that don't get many people playing them; because these machines do not pay off as frequently as machines that are continually played (busy).

PLAYING SLOT MACHINES

If you do not have a lot of money to invest in playing, you could start with a small sum and work yourself up to larger amounts. In other words begin with a nickel machine, advance to a quarter and, then, to the dollar machine — if you've been winning enough to afford that type of play. Many people start with a small amount of money (one coin at a time) to test how the machine is paying (either slow and not getting anything, or fast and winning some money). Then you could, either put more money into a machine (if it's hot) or change machines (if it's cold). If perhaps, after three plays, and you're only getting small amounts of money in return, you get a psychic feeling (hunch) to move to another slot machine — follow your instincts.

Single lines on Multiple coin slot machines, in the long run, cost more to play; you'll only receive a small return if you play a small amount (the single line). Therefore, if this is all you want to play, you are better off avoiding a Multiple-slot machine. If you play the maximum amount of coins (like nine lines), your chances to win are improved because you can hit many lines at one time in various ways. That's when you can increase your winnings. But keep in mind, you can lose a lot faster by spending more money on these Multiple-line slot machines. There are many people who play fifty nickels at a time on the Multiple-line machines — some have lost plenty; others have won big.

There is a credit meter on slot machines which some players use as they accumulate wins rather than collecting their winnings after each game. Thus, the player doesn't have to insert new coins — and I've noticed that these people win bigger than those who cash out after each game they've won. Perhaps, those who cash out after each game they've won, they like to hear the jingling of the coins as they come out of the machine. Maybe, it makes them think they won big or they could feel free to move to another machine if that one doesn't continue to win. Believe it or not, but there are lots of people who do not know about the building of credits on a slot machine!

REGULAR SLOT MACHINES

The regular slot machines are the Blazing Sevens (777), fruits (like cherries), Double Diamonds, etc., Those who do not know how to play the Video Poker machines usually play the regular slot machines. Or people who don't want to "think" and make decisions, prefer to play a machine that they can hit the spin button and win or lose. People can win enormous sums of money on them; especially, the dollar and five-dollar machines. In Las Vegas these machines are popular with the tourists and pay off (sometimes) more than Video Poker machines on the strip (main street where the most luxurious casinos are located). The locals play mostly Video Poker Machines in residential area casinos. These machines pay off bigger than regular slot machines. But, regardless of what you play, you can still lose or win. If a regular slot machine indicated someone won a jackpot, most players stay clear of those machines. However, I've seen the regular slot machines pay off continually in one night, because some slot machines are computerized to pay off frequently. Also, because there has been a steady stream of people playing them. Some people believe that the more money you invest in a machine, the bigger it will pay off. Often, this is true — however, I've seen people put hundreds of dollars into slot machines and walk away losers.

VIDEO POKER SLOT MACHINES

The Video Poker slot machine gives you longer playtime, and pays off more frequently than regular slot machines. These computer-generated machines are programmed with fifty-two cards, which are shuffled within the machine. Five cards at a time are dealt on the screen (unless you are playing a Multiple-line video poker machine). The player has the option to discard any or all of the original cards shown on the screen. You can take your time to decide which cards to keep (hold) and which should be discarded (the button is beneath the card on the screen); thus, the cards that the player wants to hold remain and new cards appear. Then the player checks the hand shown on the screen to see if he/she has a winning combination. A CANCEL button is pressed if the player wants to restore a discarded card. The DRAW button is pressed for the second time and the slot machine will show new cards on the screen. (These new cards replace the cancelled ones.)

If a player wins the first time cards show up on the screen, the player presses all five HOLD buttons then pushes down the DRAW button. If the player wins, the slot machine pays off. After each game, the cards are re-shuffled (within the machine — computer-generated) for the next game. All the player notices is new cards coming up each time he/she plays (the shuffling and reshuffling is not seen by the player — it's not visible on the screen. Note: WARNING — The player has to be very careful that a winning hand is not discarded. Do not play fast or you could make a mistake. When you press a HOLD button, look at the screen (before pressing the DRAW button) and see if the words HOLD are still lit on the screen above the card, or cards, you wish to HOLD. Some machines don't work as well as others, and I've seen the HOLD button go on and off and, thus, the player lost because he/she pressed the DRAW button too fast.

There are many varieties of Video Poker Machines: Draw Poker, Bonus Poker, Double Bonus Poker, Double Double Bonus Poker, Triple Poker, Triple Play Poker, Kings or Better Poker, The Joker is Wild, Deuces Wild, Loose Deuces, Four of A Kind, Progressive, Double-Up and so on.

PAY OFFS

Always look at the various Video Poker machine's pay off schedule, given on the machine, and compare the pay offs before playing a machine. The Progressive machines pay off handsomely. Double Double Bonus pays off the best. The Draw Poker and Joker is Wild don't pay much, but can pay off more frequently than other machines. The Loose Deuces machine pays plenty. Many people play the Double Bonus Video Poker slot machine; it derives its name (Double Bonus) because it will pay more than the regular Bonus machines, or many other Video Poker slot machines when it comes to the higher bracket of pay offs such as Four of a Kind, Straight Flush, Full House or Flush. The least amount of pay off is listed first, and the highest amount of pay off is listed last: Jacks or Better (one Pair), Two Pair, Straight, Three of a Kind, Flush, Full House, Four of a Kind, Straight Flush, Four Aces, The Royal Flush. NOTE: These are the only hands that give you a return on your money; in other words, they are the only combinations that pay off.

When you want to play a Progressive slot machine, look above the machine to see how much the money is up to (every second the amount changes). If it is up to a high figure, play it to get a big payoff. They pay off better than other jackpot machines, but less frequently. If the Progressive machine has accumulated a small amount that implies that it paid off recently; therefore, it is unlikely to pay off again. It starts off big, and as players put money into the progressive machines, the amount it pays off increases — only to go down to a small sum, once a player wins the jackpot. If you continually return to the same casino, keep your eyes on the amount it rises to (and pays off with, when someone wins), and when it is down to a low figure. Thus, you can judge when you should give it a try.

It is in your best interest to always play the maximum coins (if you can afford it), because your chances to win big are much better. Depending upon the machine you play or the casino or country you play in — maximum amounts vary from 5 to 50 coins. If you play a small amount, let's say one quarter on a Quarter Video Poker Machine — and you get a Royal Flush (the highest pay combination), all you would win is 250 quarters, which equals $62.50. However, if you play the maximum amount of five quarters, and you get a Royal Flush, you'd win $1,000. It would be a real heartbreaker, if you didn't have the maximum coins in because Royal Flush's are rare.

Note: Warning: If you put the maximum amount of coins in a machine, be careful not to touch (press) any buttons. Most machines automatically pop up with a hand (when you put the maximum amount of coins in the machine). If you press a button (especially the DEAL button) before letting them pop up automatically, you could lose the maximum bet you just put into the machine. Let's say that five quarters is the maximum amount to bet on a quarter machine. If you press the DEAL/DRAW button without thinking, your game is over and you didn't have a chance to HOLD any cards.

PLAYING POKER

Live poker and Video Poker Slot Machines are the same, except you are playing with a computer-generated machine not other people. The suits are Clubs, Spades, Hearts and Diamonds. The Ace is used as a low (numbered) straight (A-2-3-4-5) or high (numbered) straight (10-J-Q-K-A). The low cards are 2, 3, 4, 5, 6, 7, 8, 9, and 10. The high cards are Ace, King, Queen, and Jack. When playing Video Poker the idea is to get a combination that will pay off (those combinations that Pay Off are listed on the machine in the PAY OFFS section. Look at the screen on the Video Poker slot machine because it will tell you if you have any winning combinations (Jacks or Better, Two Pair, Straight, Three of a Kind, Flush, Full House, Four of a Kind, Straight Flush, Four Aces or Royal Flush). Do *NOT* keep the Kicker (one Jack, one Queen, One King or one Ace) IF YOUR OTHER CARDS ARE LOW (NUMBERED) CARDS.

THE VARIOUS COMBINATIONS

Jacks or Better (One Pair): A pair of Jacks, a pair of Queens, a pair of Kings, a pair of Aces (the lowest pair is

Jacks, followed by Queens, Kings and Aces — the highest pair). If you keep getting Jacks or Better (and nothing else) on the machine — change machines.

Two Pair: Different pairs of different suits (hearts, diamonds, spades, clubs), but of similar denominations. For instance: Two cards with an eight (one is eight of clubs, the other is the eight of spades) and two other cards in the hand with a six (one is six of hearts, the other is six of clubs). When holding Two Pairs, such as card numbers below the Jack (2, 3, 4, 5, 6, 7, 8, 9,10), there is a possibility that you will draw a third card to match the pair. This produces a better pay off (better than the Two Pair pay off) because it could produce a Full House.

Three of a Kind: Three of a Kind denotes three cards of the same denomination (number) or Three picture cards (Jack, Queen or King) or Three Aces. For example: Three cards with the number 5, regardless of suit (spades, clubs, hearts, diamonds). If you get Three of a Kind, discard the other cards and go for Four of a Kind which is a very good pay off.

Straight: Five cards in sequence, but not of the same suit. If you have four of the five cards needed (to make a straight), and the one card missing is in the *middle* of the sequence, it is best NOT to draw for that card. It is more difficult to catch a card in the *middle* than it is to catch a card at either end. To go for the *middle* card, you only have four chances to draw. If you draw (go) for the Straight at either end, you have eight chances to draw the card you need; therefore, it is smart to draw a new hand and discard (press the Cancel button) all the other cards (do not press the HOLD button down on any of the cards).

However, if you have four of the five cards in sequence (order) such as, 4, 5, 6, 7 or say 9, 10, Jack or Queen — it is advisable to hold the cards in sequence and then draw for the one card you need for the Straight — because it is open on both ends of the sequence, then your chances to get a Straight are vastly improved.

BET TO WIN *BY LYNNE PALMER*

Flush: Any five cards in the same suit, regardless of the sequence. Example: Five Diamonds, numbers 2, 3, 5, 7 and 9. If you have a Flush with say 6, 10, Queen, King, Ace of Hearts — you should definitely disregard (press the Cancel button) the Flush you have in your hand (on the screen). You should discard (press the Cancel button) and HOLD the other cards and go for the Royal Flush (the highest payoff on a Video Poker machine). A Flush only pays 8 to 1, whereas if you discard the 6 of Hearts and draw the Jack of Hearts, you'd collect 250 to 1. If you had the maximum amount of coins (5), in the slot machine, with such a bet on a quarter machine, you would win $1,000; if a dollar machine, you'd win $4,000.

Full House: Three cards of a kind and two cards of a kind. Example: Three Aces and two Fours or three Fives and two Jacks. Usually, a machine goes down after a Full House. Many players cash out. However, if it doesn't go down for three plays, it's best to stay. Some players, play a lesser amount right after the Full House for several plays and then go back up to the maximum amount, while continuing on the same machine.

Straight Flush: Five consecutive numbered cards in the same suit. Example: 4, 5, 6, 7 and 8 of Diamonds. A Straight Flush on most machines pays 50 to 1; if you bet the maximum of five coins, you get back 250 coins. Often, the Straight Flush pays more than Four of a Kind — and, then, on some machines it pays less than Four of a Kind.

Four of a Kind: Four numbered cards of the same sequence. Example: four Aces, four Queens or four Eights. Four of a Kind, from 5 to Kings, pays less than Four of a Kind, from 2 through 4. Four Aces pay more than anything.

Royal Flush: A 10, Jack, Queen, King and Ace of the same suit. If you bet under five coins, the Royal Flush will pay 250 to 1; if you bet the maximum of five coins, the Royal Flush pays 400 to 1. Everyone wants to win a Royal Flush since it pays higher than anything else in Video Poker. If you win a Royal Flush on a Progressive machine, it will pay even more (look at top of machine to see what it pays as it varies).

If you have a 10 and a picture card (Jack, Queen, King), it's wise to hold them in case you get a Royal Flush, but make sure the 10 and picture card is the same suit (both hearts, diamonds, spades or clubs). If you have 2 or 3 picture cards come up (on the screen), hold them both. When 2 Pairs come up or 2 Ace's , hold them both.

If a 10 and 2 picture cards (of a different suit) come up, discard the 10. If a 10, Jack, Queen or King of the same suit appears on the screen, hold them — perhaps, you'll get a Royal Flush.

If a 10, Jack or Queen of the same suit comes up and a King of a different suit comes up — discard the King (of the different suit) — perhaps, you'll get a Royal Flush.

DEUCES WILD AND JOKER IS WILD VIDEO POKER SLOT MACHINES

These two machines are similar: The Joker is the Wild card on the Joker is Wild Machine; the Deuce is Wild on the Deuces Wild machine. These machines pay on a semi-regular basis more frequently than other types of slot machines. Also you play longer (get more play-time for your money) than any other type of Regular or Video Poker Slot Machine. The Deuces Wild slot machine pays with consistency. In fact, I've seen people win so much on these machines that the casino put them out of service for several days. Or they are moved to a new location; thus, get the model number of the machine so you can locate it, if it's been moved.

The Deuce's Wild machine is played almost the same as a regular Video Poker slot machine. The exception is the Deuce (two) is Wild and can be substituted for whatever you need to get a winning hand. On The Joker is Wild machine, the Joker is Wild and can be substituted for whatever you need to get a winning hand.

When you play the Deuce's Wild machine, and you get three Deuces, discard all the cards (except the three Deuces) and go for the fourth Deuce. If you get Four Deuces, it pays 250 to 1, which if you have five coins (the maximum bet) in — and it's a quarter machine — you'll be paid $250.00. If it's a dollar machine, and you have five coins in, you'll be paid $2,500.00

If two Deuces show up on the screen, discard the other three cards as long as it is not a big pay off — and go for the Four Deuces. Also, on this machine, you may get a "Wild Royal Flush" which pays 25 to 1 — the screen will flash the words "Royal Flush with Deuces." If you get a Royal Flush without the deuces, and you have five coins (quarters) in, you will win $1,000. If you are playing the dollar machine and have five coins (dollars) in, you'll win $4,000 — if you get a Royal Flush without the deuces.

DOUBLE-UP MACHINES

Many Video Poker Machines offer you the opportunity to double your money after a win. You may double as many times as you wish until you lose or keep winning. This is when your Intuition, sixth sense, ESP, hunch, instinct, gut feeling or psychic ability can be utilized to the fullest. If you do not want to double up, press the HOLD button on the far right. If you want to double up, press the HOLD button on the far left. (The screen will ask you, "Do you want to double up? — Yes, or No?")

If you Double up, a card will appear face up on the left side (that's the dealer's card). The other four cards will remain face down. Use your gut feelings and select the card you think will be higher than the dealer's card by pressing the button in front of it (your chosen, gut feeling card). If your card is a lower card (than the dealer's) you lose; if your card is higher, you win. If your card is the same card (a tie) as the dealer's — it's a draw (tie), and the game can proceed as normal. To get a lot of money you have to win many double-ups in succession — but stop before you lose. Remember, that you can't win every time.

HOW TO TELL WHEN
YOU'RE GOING TO LOSE

When a machine is hot (almost every play is a win), stay with that machine. Put more money in (or the maximum) if the machine is escalating on an upward trend (your money is increasing). Perhaps, this is a machine that pays off more frequently than others.

If you receive small returns on your money, especially after playing a slot machine for a long time, change machines. Some machines only go to a certain amount and then start downward to take you out. They are all programmed differently. Play fewer coins if you are losing (the machine is on a downward escalation, i.e., your money is decreasing) — that is, if you want to continue playing at that same slot machine.

Once you've won a Royal Flush, Four of a Kind, Straight Flush or Full House, the Video Poker machine starts to escalate downward (your money decreases). If it is a hot machine and escalates downward after you've gotten Four of a Kind, the Straight Flush or Full House — and goes back up again after one or two times of getting nothing — then stick with the machine because it could pay off again.

Most Video Poker machines (except the Deuce's Wild) will take you out (make you lose) on a gradual basis. They have teasers to keep you playing. You could go up, then down and back up — eventually, these machines escalate down and you've lost. Often when you're on your last coin (or coins) you may get teased with a Straight or Full House (sometimes even Three of a Kind) — but then you'll gradually go downward. In other words, you'll win then lose and keep this up for awhile. Keep in mind that these machines are computerized and programmed by an expert.

Some people, when the machine is escalating downward, and get a Full House — cash out after they've gotten a Full House. If the slot machine lets you win once with your last coin (coins) — it's likely to make you lose the next time (play). Use logic and analyze the machine, as you're playing. Keep track of how many times you didn't get anything (and went downward). I can watch people play and know when they are going to lose. It never fails — the exception is on the Deuce's Wild machine; it takes you down gradually, but keeps you winning and playing longer, before it takes you out.

If after FOUR times a regular or Video Poker slot machine (except the Deuce's Wild machine) takes you down (you don't get ONE winning hand after four plays) then the machine is going to gradually escalate downward and take you out if you continue to play it. I have watched for over five hours a night for ten years and analyzed all the machines and do a countdown to see if after FOUR TIMES NOTHING WAS WON — and it has never failed — they end up losing. The Deuces Wild machine takes you down at least SEVEN times before you start really escalating downward and out. Therefore, after Four Times of not getting a winning hand — CHANGE MACHINES OR QUIT PLAYING.

CHAPTER NINE
ROULETTE

Stand in a casino and look in the direction of the roulette tables; if there is more than one, go to the table that catches your eye or that you've got a good gut feeling about. Mentally say (as you are approaching the table), "Make me a winner!" Most people guess at numbers, which is using their ESP (without realizing it); they get a "feel" for a number (numbers). Always stick with your first impressions (those numbers that first pop out of your mind: intuition). Many players are upset when they don't follow their first impression (and would have won had they done so). You can use your Lucky Numbers (see Chapter Three). Or play your favorite numbers (birthdays, house or apartment number, license plate or telephone numbers, dates when important events occurred, i.e., anniversaries).

In Las Vegas there are many casinos that have an automatic screen that is lit up with the 16 numbers that just came in. Many times, I've noticed that three times a 33 came up — and sure enough, it came up again. Numbers, like winning and losing, run in cycles. If you are at a table that does not have this automatic screen (like European casinos) then keep a notepad and watch the numbers that come up for awhile, before you start playing. Keep in mind that if you play long enough, you'll end up losing.

When playing roulette, visualize the ball rolling on the number (numbers — most people bet many numbers at one time) you have wagered, or if you've bet on something else on the roulette table, such as a red or black number — then, visualize that color winning. Mentally say, "Let the ball roll on — (whatever you wagered)."

Most casinos have a plaque on the roulette table (or sign) that tells the would be player the minimum and maximum bet (the amount of chips) a player needs to play the game. These vary from casino to casino as well as from country to country. When in doubt ask the dealer (croupier) at the roulette table. This amount involves the inside and outside numbers on the roulette table.

CHIPS

Buy the chips from the dealer (croupier); if your lucky color is available, ask for that color. If you don't know your lucky color, ask for yellow (rules "ready cash" in astrology) or green (the color of money in most countries). When you quit, and you still have chips left, turn them in to the dealer (croupier) who'll pay you their worth in casino chips — take those chips to the cashier's cage and have them exchanged for cash.

THE WHITE BALL

Just before the actual game starts, the dealer (croupier) takes the white roulette ball and starts it rolling around the inside rim of the wheel — the ball is spun counter to the wheel's motion. The dealer (croupier) will say, or motion with a swing of the hands over the table, "No more bets." At that point, you cannot place any more chips on the table. The ball spins and falls into a slot (pocket) which corresponds to a number and a color (red or black). The dealer (croupier) places on the table a marker to indicate the winning number (and color of number is there too. The loser's chips are taken off the table and the dealer (croupier) pays the winner in more chips.

LAYOUT — OUTSIDE TABLE BETS

In the USA and Europe the locations of these outside bets differ; however, it's easy to see their differences — when in doubt, ask the dealer (croupier). You can bet on either red or black (as winning), odd or even, high or low (the low are numbers from 1 to 18; high are numbers from 19 to 36 — if the winning number falls between one of these, and you bet it, you win) — all of these bets are "even-money" bets.

Note: In Nevada casinos: If you bet any of the preceding and the winning number is zero (0) or zero zero (00) — you lose your entire bet. In Atlantic City, New

Jersey, you lose half of your bet. In Europe: Casinos only have one zero (0). A player has two options: (a) You can make a deal (called "Partage") to give up half of your bet. (b) You can go for one more spin of the roulette wheel, then, if zero (0) comes up again you lose; however, if red-black, or odd-even or low-high comes in (and you've bet one of them), you've won.

Dozen Bets: On the outside section of the table, you'll see three sections called "Dozens." The first dozen are numbers from 1 to 12; the second dozen are numbers from 13 to 24; the third dozen are numbers from 25 to 36. You can bet on as many dozen numbers as you want; perhaps, you want to bet on both the first dozen and the third dozen at the same time (then if the winning number falls into either one of these categories, you'll win "even money." In other words, you are covering 24 numbers out of 36 numbers.

Column Bets: You can bet on which column (row) you think that the winning number will fall in; thus, you cover 12 numbers on a single bet. Column wins pay 2 to 1. Note: The zero (0) or zero zero (00) are NOT IN-CLUDED in a Column (row) bet. If a zero (0) or zero zero (00) wins, you lose. You can bet on two columns (rows) at the same time, if you want.

LAYOUT — INSIDE TABLE BETS

These are the numbers found in each of the three rows (columns), including zero (0) and zero zero (00).

Single Bets: A "Single number bet" is a bet on a single zero (0), double zero (00), or any single number from 1 through 36. If you win, the payoff is 35 to 1. You can bet as many single numbers as you want. The chips are placed in the middle where the number is located (the square's center). More than one player can bet the same number as you; remember everyone has chips in different colors; therefore you, and the dealer (croupier), know which colors are yours and which are the other players. Chips of different players, playing the same number, are placed on top of each other. You must place the minimum amount of chips in this numbered section of the layout table. If you don't the dealer (croupier) will advise you accordingly.

Three-Number Bets: This is a bet covering three numbers at one time with 1 chip (or more, if you like). Center the chip (chips) on the line which divides the left number from the spaces marked 1st 12, or 2nd 12 or 3rd 12 (in other words, place the chip (chips) on the line separating the "dozens" betting area from the columns of numbers. (You'll have 3 consecutive numbers you're betting on). This wager pays off at 11 to 1.

Four-Number Bets: A bet place on any four numbers in a square; however, place a chip (chips) exactly where the lines intersect at between these four numbers. This wager pays off 8 to 1.

Five-Number Bets: This bet cannot be made in European casinos. This is considered the worst bet in roulette. These five-numbered bets are made only where the single zero (0), double zero (00) and the numbers 1, 2 and 3 appear on the roulette table. Place a chip (chips) on the outer corner of the dividing line between zero (0) and 1 — if in doubt, ask the dealer (croupier). You are wagering that the winning number will be 0, 00, 1, 2 or 3. This wager pays off 6 to 1.

Six-Number Bets: You are betting six numbers at one time; these numbers are any two consecutive groups of 3 numbers. The player places a chip (chips) on the outer line intersection between two groups of three numbers. In other words, place the chip (chips) on the *outside* dividing line that separates the "dozen bets" from the *inside* numbers; place the chip (chips) on the dividing line *between* two numbers (in the column-row section) and the "dozens section." Example: You place a chip (chips)

ROULETTE TABLE LAYOUT

on the 2nd dozen line in the center where the dividing line is. Place your chip on the middle (center), for instance, between 13 and 16 (inside section), *but* on the outer left line's edge by the 2nd dozen's section. Thus, you win if any of these numbers come up — 13, 14, 15, 16, 17 or 18 (six numbers). This wager pays off 5 to 1.

SPLITTING YOUR BETS

A multiple number bet is called a split bet. This is when you place a chip (chips) on the dividing line between two numbers, including zero (0) and zero zero (00). Thus, the wager covers both numbers and if one of the numbers wins, the pay off is 17 to 1. The majority of people play split bets. You can play as many split bets as you want in a game, but a line must separate these two numbers.

If you want to make a corner bet, place a chip at the point (center) where all four numbers meet. This is a popular bet. If you win, the wager pays off 8 to 1.

You can also place a chip (chips) on any of the lines which separate a column and the "dozens area" (on outside of the three columns). Thus, this covers the outside column and the three numbers in the three columns directly across from it. For example: You place a chip (chips) on the 3rd dozen section (so you can bet on the line between it and the numbers 25, or 28, 31 or 34; thus, if the winning number is 32, you win because the line by the number 31, and 3rd dozen, covers numbers 31, 32 and 33 — therefore, if any of these numbers come in, you win). The wager pays off 11 to 1.

EUROPEAN CASINOS

I have played roulette in various casinos throughout Europe. The first time I saw a roulette table there; I was shocked, because the layout differed from those in the USA. The games are run by Croupiers. For pay offs a rake is used to collect and pay off chips. You cannot make a 5 number bet because the table does not have a double zero (00).

The Outside layout has been shifted (in different place than the tables in the USA) and are marked:

The Dozen Bets: P-12 (Premiere, means 1st dozen) are numbers 1 to 12.

M-12 (Moyenne, means middle 2nd dozen) are numbers 13 to 24.

D-12 (Derniere, means last for 3rd dozen) numbers 25 to 36.

They have various bets that are "special," called Voisins which refers to neighboring numbers. They can be any number on a wheel, including the number you choose and two numbers on either side of them; thus, it takes five chips to bet that way. Or you can make a Nine chip bet, called "Voisins du zero" — which is 8 chips bet on splits and 1 chip bet on the Three numbered bet.

CHAPTER TEN
BLACKJACK

When you enter a casino, look for the section where the Blackjack tables are located. Select the table that catches your eye (the one you have a good "gut feeling" or instinct about). Blackjack is played at a semi-circular table with six or seven chairs (one for each player). The dealer stands behind the table.

There's a small plaque (sign) at each table that indicates the minimum or maximum amount of money you can bet. Often, the casino's rules appear on the plaque. Many tables have the rules printed on the felt surface in sections where the player places chips on the table. On the table there are six or seven circles or squares for each player to bet on. Never hand your money to a dealer; place your money on the table next to the circle or square in front of you. Do NOT put money inside the circle or square; this area is used only for making bets. Ask the dealer to change your money into chips ($1, $5, $25, $100, $500). Cash in chips at the casino's cashier's cage where you've played. Place your chip bet in the square or circle on the table in front of you.

Choosing Your Seat: The cards are dealt by the dealer in a clockwise fashion. The first player to receive the cards sits to the left of the dealer; last person to receive the cards, sits to the right of the dealer. You could be the only one at the table; however, other players can join the table while you're playing. Many players like to be the last one to receive the cards; therefore, they can study the cards the others hold and the decisions they make, and do "card counting" (explained later in this chapter).

The Cards: Single or multiple (three or more, such as six) decks of cards may be used. A single deck is composed of 52 cards. There are four suits (hearts, diamonds, clubs, spades) and they have no value (as suits). In each suit, there is a 2, 3, 4, 5, 6, 7,8, 9, 10, Jack, Queen, King and Ace. The numbered cards are counted as the number they contain (I'll call them points); their number is their value. The Jack, Queen and King are counted as 10 points. The Ace is counted as either 1 point or 11 points.

After the dealer shuffles the cards they are cut by a player or dealer (with single deck only). Once cut, the dealer takes the top card (face up) and puts it at the bottom of the deck, or it's placed in a plastic case to the right of the dealer face down. In that case, then, the discarded cards are placed on top of that card. However, if the card is face up at bottom of the deck, all discarded cards during a game play are placed face up below that card. NOTE: When multiple decks are used, the cards are not cut. The cards come out of a shoot when multiple decks are used. The dealer then deals cards from the shoot (plastic case) and cards are dealt face up to each player. The purpose of multiple decks of cards is so a player cannot count cards.

THE GAME: Each player tries to beat the dealer, not each other. Two cards are dealt, by the dealer (one at a time) to every player (while this is happening, mentally say, "Bring me cards that'll make me win." The dealer's second card is turned face up. Thus, all players can see the dealer's card. It is impossible for a player to lose (go over 21 points) with the first two cards dealt by the dealer. Thus, the highest point is 21, followed by 20, 19, 18, etc. To win Blackjack, your cards points should total 21 or as close to 21 as you can get. If your cards total points go over 21 points, you lose and must immediately turn all of your cards over to show the dealer that you've lost (gone over 21 points). At that moment your cards and chips are taken from you (by the dealer). Even if the dealer loses and you, also, are over 21 points — you still lose. If the dealer loses (goes over 21 points), all bets are paid off at even money (1 to 1), except in the case of Blackjack which is paid 18 to 1. If you get cards that total UNDER 21 points and your total points are higher than the dealer's total points, you win and get paid even-money. If the dealer is the only one to get a Blackjack, the dealer wins even-money and all other players lose. If you get UNDER 21 points and the dealer's total points are higher than yours, you lose. If player and dealer both hold the same amount of points, they are tied — neither one wins even if you both have 21 points. *Note:* BLACKJACK can only be achieved with two cards, the Ace and either a ten, Jack, Queen or King. If you have a Blackjack, the dealer pays you 1 1/2 to win. If you get a total of 21 points AND DO NOT HAVE AN ACE WITH EITHER A TEN, JACK, QUEEN — then you get paid even-money.

Dealer has one card face up and if it's 10, Jack, Queen or King — then, dealer looks at the face down card to see if it is an Ace (which, if it is, would total to 21 points and be Blackjack). If this occurs, other players lose, unless they also have Blackjack (21 points). If the dealer has Blackjack, the players still in the game will be asked if they want INSURANCE (which is dealt with later in this chapter). With a single deck, if in your original hand (the first two cards dealt to you), you have 21 points — then, immediately turn over your cards (hand) and you're paid right away — that is if the dealer does NOT have Blackjack.

Once all players have their two cards (dealt by the dealer), the player must decide (before the dealer gets to you) whether you are going to be "hit" or "stay." If you don't make that decision, the dealer will pass by you. Should you "hit" or stand (stay)? The player should look at the dealers 1st face up card; if the dealer has a higher total than player AND player's card is low enough to take a risk (like 13 to 16 points) — that's when player may chance a "hit." Thus, a "hit" depends on your total points and the total points of the dealer's face up card. The worst cards for a dealer is to have a 4, 5 or 6 face up (a dealer then has to draw cards that could make the dealer go over 21 points). You can have as many cards "hit" as you want, but be careful you don't go over 21 points. A "hit" means you're asking the dealer for another card.

If the dealer has a total of 7 points (a seven) face up and your cards total 12 points, you may want to have a hit until you reach 17 points. However, if you get a card that counts as ten points, you'll be over 21 and lose. If your cards total 12 points and the dealer has a 4, 5, or 6 face up, STAY on 12. If your hand totals less than 15 points and the dealer's face up card is 7 points or 8, 9, 10 or Jack, Queen, King — ask for a "hit." If you have a total of 14 points or more and the dealer's face up card is a 2, 3, 4, 5 or 6 STAY (STAND). Stay or Stand (same thing) is when a player is satisfied with the total points held and, thus, stays put.

BET TO WIN *BY LYNNE PALMER*

If a player's cards total points are low (like 4 and 5, which totals 9 points), the player will want to be "hit" with another card. If a Jack, Queen or King is dealt (each is valued at 10 points) then player would have 19 points and should STAND; otherwise, player could go over 21 if a "hit" was in force. If an Ace is dealt, then player's total points could be 20 (counting the Ace as 1 point) — but that's risky to try. You can decide, when you have an Ace, whether you'll count it as 1 or 11 points.

SIGNALS: There is no verbal communication between you and the dealer. This is a silent game played by signals. If you want a "hit," pick up your two original cards and scrape the edges of the card (toward yourself) against the felt surface on top of the table. If you want another "hit," the same process is repeated. Or gently scratch the felt surface on the table with a motion toward you or flick with your hand or finger toward you.

If you want to "Stay" ("stand"), because you're satisfied with the cards (points) you hold, slide those cards under the chips you bet and DO NOT touch the chips or cards again. Or you could wave your hand (with palm down) sideways. *If the game is played with A Multiple Deck:* If a "hit" is desired, player points index fingers at the cards, or may scratch felt surface of table top (the scratch is done behind player's cards and with index finger). If player wants to "stand" ("stay"), player waves hands over the cards with the palm down and the game continues.

SPLIT PAIRS: In your Original deal (when dealer dealt you two cards) and those two cards are the same pair (two cards of different suits with the same number, i.e., the two cards are both numbered "6" which equals 12 points). If you want to take those two cards and play two hands (two different games) at the same time — then, you must spend extra chips (money) and both hands must be covered by a bet with the same amount of money as the original bet.

BET TO WIN *BY LYNNE PALMER*

Player draws cards on the first (original) hand (say a "6") until player is satisfied. Then player draws cards on the second hand (the other "6") and continues to be "hit" or decides to "stand." All cards that represent 10 points (the 10, Jack, Queen, King) — do NOT SPLIT. If you split an Ace, only ONE additional card will be dealt, to each Ace you hold in your original hand. Never split two pairs that are numbered 4 or two that are numbered 5 because with the two four's you have 8 points and with the two five's you have 10 points and if you draw a card that's valued at 10 points — you'd have 18 points or 20 points.

DO YOU WANT TO DOUBLE DOWN?

If you want to double your bet on your first (original) hand, you can. If you do, the dealer will only give you ONE more additional card. Various casinos in the USA, and other countries, have different rules on what point value can or cannot be Doubled Down. Always ask the dealer. If you decide to Double Down, you must turn over your face down cards (if playing with a single deck) and put a bet on them; the bet has to be equal to your original bet. If your cards were dealt face up, you make an additional bet (multiple decks). *Note:* If your two cards total 11 points, it would be more logical to go "down for double" which means you double your bet and are dealt another card (only one card) to go with the 11.

INSURANCE

A player can insure a bet, if the dealer asks, "Insurance?" then, the player can bet up to 1/2 of the original bet. The player is betting that the dealer has a 10 point value card face down (underneath the face up card on top)… and it is possible that the UNDERNEATH card is an ACE which means the dealer has BLACKJACK (21 points).

If the dealer has Blackjack, the player who got Insurance is paid off at 2 to 1, *but the player's original bet is lost*. Therefore, it's a standoff between player and dealer. In other words, when a player makes an insurance bet and player is right, player wins the bet; however if player is wrong, players loses the money that was bet on insurance and the game continues.

SURRENDER OR NOT TO SURRENDER?

Some casinos have surrender policies, others do not; ask a dealer if that casino where you're playing allows "surrender." If allowed, a player can forfeit 1/2 of the original bet if the player decides NOT TO PLAY THE ORIGINAL HAND (first two cards dealt) against the dealer. Why would a player want to surrender?

Suppose the player notices that the dealer's face-up card has a 10 point value, which means that the dealer *could have* a higher total with the card face-down (underneath the face-up card, which player can not see). Perhaps the player has a total point value of 15, and player cannot decide whether to "hit" or "stand." If player took a "hit" and the next card had a 10-point value, player could lose (because that 10 and 15 points would be over 21). However, if player "stands" — the 15 points is not that high, but it's risky to chance the dealer who could get an Ace (which would be Blackjack for the dealer) and the player would lose. Or perhaps the dealer's face-down card is a 6, 7, 8, 9 or 10 point value which implies that the dealer's total point value beats your 15 point value, then you'd lose. Therefore, you decide to surrender (give up your hand, if allowed in that casino) and you'd then only lose 1/2 of your bet instead of the entire bet.

If the dealer has a face up card valued at 10 points and you have as your total points 16 — then surrender. Give up 16 points if dealer's face-up card is an Ace. However, do not give up two cards numbered 8 — instead split them.

CARD COUNTING

Note: Card counting cannot be done if you are playing with multiple decks. If you are experienced and have a good memory, card counting (keeping track of the cards with single deck only) can help you win. However, you still have to be lucky and have the right cards dealt to you. If mostly smaller numbered (such as numbers from 2 to 7) cards have shown up, then that's favorable for you. The more fives that have shown up (been used), the easier it is for the dealer to lose. That implies that there are many higher numbered cards left in the deck; thus, if the dealer draws these higher numbered cards it makes it easier for the dealer to go over 21 points.

If you notice many Ace's or cards valued at ten points (ten, Jack, Queen, King) *coming out in the game,* chances are you won't get a Blackjack. If you notice that there are more Aces and cards valued at ten points (ten, Jack, Queen, King) *still left in the deck* (because they have not been showing up), bet more money. However, if there are NOT many Aces and cards valued at ten points left in the single deck (because they have shown up), bet less money (because that's unfavorable for the player). During the game, increase or decrease your bet depending upon whether you think you're going to win or not win.

BOOKS BY LYNNE PALMER

ASTROLOGICAL ALMANAC (Annual)

Plan your life day-by-day. No math needed or knowledge of astrology. *Part One:* Sun sign sections features colors, numbers, gems, music, flowers, perfume, books, herbs, gifts, cities and countries, yearly forecast, best days for sex and much more. *Part Two:* There are 500 categories to plan your life such as best and avoid dates for surgery, dental work or travel by air; dates when to beautify, sign contracts, open a business, start legal matters and much more. 256 pages, paperback, $20.00, plus $4.00 shipping and handling.

MONEY MAGIC

Discover how to overcome obstacles in making money. Learn how to do Magical Devices, which can bring riches. Manipulate your environment so you'll be on top. What attracts wealth according to your Sun sign? Learn about negative and positive thoughts. 124 pages, paperback, $8.95, plus $1.00 shipping and handling.

YOUR LUCKY DAYS AND NUMBERS

Two types of Numerology — discover your lucky days to gamble, when not to gamble, invest, marry, divorce and much more. Your Lucky numbers for gambling, your home address, phone number and much more. Easy-to learn and do. 76 pages, paperback, $8.95, plus $1.00 shipping and handling.

IS YOUR NAME LUCKY FOR YOU?

Learn how to add up your name, according to numerology and astrology — perhaps, you're lucky, or unlucky, because of your name vibration. Are you vibrating to several mixed vibrations because you are called by several names? How to change your name and, thus, change your life. A name can mean the difference between success and failure, or between happiness and misery. 240 pages, paperback, $18.00, plus $4.00 shipping and handling.

PROSPERITY

Discover about investments and how you should handle your money. Information about 65 investments. Over 21 magical devices, which could attract more money into your life. A Sun sign section on money and investments. Learn how to avoid problems and to capitalize on your strong points. Make the decisions that lead to success. 254 pages, paperback, $20.00, plus $4.00 shipping and handling.

ARE YOU COMPATIBLE WITH YOUR BOSS, PARTNER, COWORKER, CLIENTS, EMPLOYEES?

The way you relate, handle and deal with others could be the difference between your being successful or losing out. An astrological guide to compatibility in business. What your real assets are and how to make them pay off. How to read your clients and make them the one offer they can't refuse. Being in the right place at the right time. 240 pages, paperback, $20.00, plus $4.00 shipping and handling.

SPECIAL REPORT — THE USA UNDER ATTACK

Information about the future of the USA — the economy, stock market, and terrorists. The USA horoscope until the year 2007. New York City Horoscope until the year 2005. Also included is the horoscope of Osama Bin Laden. $23.00, includes shipping and handling.

Visit Lynne Palmer's Web Site at
www.lynnepalmer.com